Scholarships 2020

5-Step Process & 10 Top Places to Find Billions in Scholarships

By

Phil Johncock, MA, MMs, GPC

Table of Contents

Preface

One of the biggest choices that you face when you want to go to college is the **choice "to get" or "not to get" a student loan to pay for your education**

In the Introduction, you will discover 8 reasons why **you don't want to fall prey to the student loan debt trap**.

Instead, in **5 simple, yet powerful steps**, *College Scholarships 2020* shows you exactly what you need to do to **get all the scholarship money you need to cover your college expenses** in 2020-21.

Chapters 1-5 are designed to walk you through a simple, yet powerful 5-step process that will help you get the grant and scholarship funding you need to start and finish your undergraduate or graduate degrees without having to take out a student loan.

Chapter 1 will show you how to create a Support Team to help you be successful. You do not have to go it all alone!

Chapter 2 will show you how to create a budget estimate for college-related expenses. Research shows that the clearer and more accurate your budget, the more likely you will find and receive scholarship money.

Chapter 3 invites you to apply for your FAFSA® for federal student aid and shows you how much you can expect to get.

Chapter 4 shows you 10 top places to find scholarship money for the school year that starts July 1, 2020 and runs through June 30, 2021.

Chapter 5 gives you a tiny step that will make a huge difference in setting you apart from the competition.

In *College Scholarships 2020*, you will discover how to **say "no" to the student loan debt trap** -- money that you have to pay back -- and instead **say "yes" to free scholarships -**- money that you don't have to pay back!

Let's get started!

Enjoy!

Phil Johncock

INTRODUCTION

The Student Loan Debt Trap

Life is like math. If it's too easy, something is wrong!

Likewise, student loans (i.e., federal, state, private, etc.) are remarkably easy to get. But, hardly anyone will tell you that "something is wrong." But, it is.

What's wrong with getting a student loan to help you pay for your college?

There at least 8 reasons why getting a student loan is wrong, even a possible debt trap:

Reason 1 - You've got to pay it back.

This is a real bummer… maybe not now, but definitely later! Since this pain of repayment is delayed, there is no discomfort up front. You feel great, right! You've basically get "free" money now for your education.

But, it's not really "free", is it! The pain and burden that you must carry is merely delayed.

Reason 2 - Student loans may stress you more than any other debt!

According to a 2019 National Tracking Poll[1], "64% of adults (polled) feel some or a lot of stress about undergraduate student loan debt, compared with 60% who feel some or a lot of stress about credit card debt; 42% who worry about mortgage debt; and 42% who feel at least some stress about car loans.

Student loan debt is not only more likely to worry adults, but it's also more likely to be the cause of major concern. In fact, 45% of adults reported feeling a lot of stress about undergraduate student loans, compared with 30% who feel a lot of concern about credit cards, 18% who worry about mortgage loans a lot, and 21% who feel a lot of stress about car loans."

Reason 3 - Student loans may affect your chances of buying a home.

According to Fortune[2], "The Federal Reserve reported that in 2014 alone, student loan debt prevented 400,000 young Americans from purchasing homes."

---

[1] www.fool.com/the-ascent/student-loans/articles/report-student-loans-stress-us-out-more-any-other-debt/

[2] fortune.com/2019/07/09/bernie-sanders-cancel-student-debt

Reason 4 - Students loans decrease your chances of starting a business.

According to Fortune[3],"Karthik Krishnan, a professor at Northeastern University who specializes in student debt, told CNBC last year that people with $30,000 in student loan debt are 11% less likely to start businesses than are those without debt."

Reason 5 - Student loans may even hurt your credit rating.

"'You do stand to see longer-term negative effects on people who can't pay off their student loans,' Federal Reserve Chair Jerome Powell told Congress in March 2018. 'It hurts their credit rating; it impacts the entire half of their economic life.'" (Source: Fortune[4])

According to a CNBC report[5], "outstanding education debt in the U.S. has eclipsed credit card and auto debt. Today the average college graduate leaves school $30,000 in the red, up from $10,000 in the 1990s, and 28% of student loan borrowers (12.6 million) are in delinquency or default."

---

[3] fortune.com/2019/07/09/bernie-sanders-cancel-student-debt
[4] Ibid.
[5] www.cnbc.com/2019/06/24/bernie-sanders-has-a-plan-to-forgive-all-student-debt.html

Reason 6 - Student loans may even follow you into retirement.

According to U.S. Representative Ilhan Omar[6], "Student loans now follow millions of Americans into *retirement*." U.S. Senator Bernie Sanders[7] adds, "In a generation hard hit by the Wall Street crash of 2008, … (it's the) absurdity of sentencing an entire generation to a lifetime of debt for the 'crime' of getting a college education."

According to Fortune[8], "Since 2004, the number of Americans 60 and over with student loan debt has more than **quintupled**—from 600,000 to 3.2 million—and tens of thousands of older borrowers have had their Social Security benefits seized by the government to pay for student loans."

Reason 7 - Student loan debt disproportionately burdens ethnic students.

According to U.S. Senator Elizabeth Warren[9], the "huge student loan debt burden … disproportionately affects people of color. African-Americans are more likely to have to borrow money to go to school, more likely to borrow

---

[6] www.cnbc.com/2019/06/24/bernie-sanders-has-a-plan-to-forgive-all-student-debt.html
[7] Ibid.
[8] Ibid.
[99]www.washingtonpost.com/politics/2019/12/20/transcript-december-democratic-debate/

more money while they're in school, and have a harder time paying it off."

Reason 8 - Colleges, Student Loan Companies & Even the Federal Government Stand to Win Big

The Student Loan Trap is basically set up and perpetuated by colleges, student loan companies and even the Federal government.

Colleges

Colleges want you to attend their institutions. By making student loans easy to get and being the middle company (receiving and distributing money), they ensure that they will have "butts in seats" that will cover their costs and even make a profit to stay in business.

Student Loan Companies

Student loan companies make a profit off you and are more likely to harass you, as a loan borrower. According to The Guardian[10], "Among the 44 million Americans who have amassed our nation's whopping $1.4 Tillion in student loan debt, a call from Navient (a spin off of Sallie Mae) can produce shivers of dread.

---

[10] www.theguardian.com/money/2017/sep/06/us-student-debt-loans-navient-sallie-mae

Often, the most vulnerable borrowers are not those with the largest debt, but low-income students, first-generation students, and students of color – especially those who may attend less prestigious schools and are less likely to quickly earn enough to repay their loans, if they graduate at all.

'These are populations who are **borrowing to go to college** or ending up without a degree, and ending up with meaningless degrees, and **are … worse off than if they had never gone to college to begin with,**' said Amy Laitinen, of the nonpartisan think-tank New America.

The power and reach of the student loan industry stacks the odds against borrowers. Navient doesn't just service federal loans, it has a hand in nearly every aspect of the student loan system. It has bought up private student loans, both servicing them and earning interest off of them.

And it has purchased billions of dollars worth of the older taxpayer-backed loans, again earning interest, as well as servicing that debt. The company also owns controversial subsidiary companies such as Pioneer Credit Recovery that stand to profit from collecting the debt of loans that go into default.

And just as banks have done with mortgages, Navient packages many of the private and pre-2010 federal loans and sells them on Wall Street as asset-backed securities."

As complaints continued to rise against Navient high-pressure tactics, the Consumer Financial Protection Bureau (CFPB) sued Navient in 2016, to which Navient replied, "'There is no expectation that the servicer will act in the interest of the consumer.' Rather, it argued, 'Navient's job was to look out for the interest of the federal government and taxpayers.'"

"Better educating teens about financial literacy before they apply to college will help reduce their dependence on student loans," says *The Guardian[11]*. "But that doesn't change how the deck is stacked for those who need them."

Federal Government

Even the Federal government stands to make money off from student loans. According to CNN Money[12], "The federal loan program was, after all, created to make college affordable for more Americans.

'That's probably one of the only things the government shouldn't make money off -- I think it's terrible that one of the only profit centers we have is student loans,' Donald Trump told *The Hill* in July (2016).

But is the government really making money off of student loans?

---

[11] www.theguardian.com/money/2017/sep/06/us-student-debt-loans-navient-sallie-mae

[12] money.cnn.com/2016/08/04/pf/college/federal-student-loan-profit/index.html

By one estimate, the federal student loan program could turn a profit of $1.6 billion in 2016, according to the Congressional Budget Office (CBO).

That's not a huge profit when you consider that the program lends out about $100 billion a year. But the CBO also projects that it would keep making money each year over the next decade."

Colleges, student loan companies and the Federal government all stand to benefit by setting up the Student Debt Trap by making it super easy for you to receive a student loan. Beware!

A student loan is like math. If it's too easy, something is wrong!

My Story

My story started even before I was born. My mom told me that before any of her five boys were born, she prayed for two things:

1. That all of her children would be of service in the world.

2. That all of her children would have the money to go to college, if they choose.

Regarding the first prayer, all of my brothers and I have all served in a variety of ways. Tom helps families who speak Spanish. Jim was in the Navy and is a leader in the church. Bill is a leader in his church with a special needs son. Mark became a youth minister and works with the elderly in nursing homes.

Me. Well, I've worked with schools and charitable nonprofits for over 40 years in Mexico, Canada and the U.S.

What about the second prayer?

Well, Jim went to school on the GI Bill. Bill got a family scholarship to go to medical school, as did Mark.

I attended four years of undergraduate studies on a full-ride football scholarship AND a full-ride academic scholarship. Of course, you can't use both rides at the same time. But, after 1 year of playing football, I hung up my cleats and instead used my academic scholarship to cover all college costs.

For my two-year masters degree studies, I received a university fellowship and a family scholarship to cover costs.

I graduated with a 4-year degree and 2-year graduate degree, completely free!

Of course, you and everyone who reads this book are different and unique. The great news is that you don't have to be a top athlete or have the best grades to get scholarships.

All you need is to commit to go to college and do your due diligence to follow the 5 steps outlined within these pages.

In this book, you will discover the 5 steps to get scholarship money you don't have to pay back...

STEP 1 - Create a Support Team

STEP 2 - Create a College Budget of Expenses

STEP 3 - Complete Your FAFSA®

STEP 4 - Find Scholarships & Apply

STEP 5 - Send "Thank You" Cards

If you follow these 5 simple steps, you will position yourself to get all the scholarship money you need.

Let's start with Chapter 1 - Create Your Support Team.

..

Chapter 1

STEP 1 - Create Your Own "Support Team"

Remember: you are not in this all alone! There are many, many people out there who want you to be successful in getting scholarships that you don't have to pay back. They want you to attend and complete college.

You may not know all of the supporters you actually have. After reading Chapter 1, you should have a better idea about who to include in your own, unique Support Team.

You want to create a unique Support Team made up of individuals who all have your back and your best interests at heart. Everyone on your team should be in full support of your educational goals.

Nay-sayers (those who may be threatened by or not supportive of you and your dreams) may test your resolve in going to college. These are the people who might say things like, "You can't do it." "You're not smart enough." "College costs too much money." "Just get a job like everyone else."

Have you met any "nay-sayers"? Perhaps these are people who like to play the role of "devil's advocate" to show you everything wrong, poke holes in your dream to go to and finish college?

It's OK to have these non-supportive persons in your life. Just do not invite them to participate in your Support Team.

On the other hand, you should invite the very best supporters to participate on your Support Team. They help you at this time of a major transition from high school to college.

Here are some people you might consider for your Support Team:

- Your High School Counselors

- Your Parents or Guardians

- Your College Financial Aid Officer

- Your Peers (Friends)

- College Alumni Group Members

- College (and High School) Student Club Members

- Reviewers (Applications & Essays)

Support Team Roles

Here are 7 specific ways your Support Team can help you…

1. They can hold your vision for college. Tell them why college is important to you. Share with them the specific subjects you would like to study and why you want to study these subjects. Share with them goals for your education and career aspirations.

2. They can hold the vision for how much you need. Tell them: "According to the college budget of expenses I created in Chapter 2, I need $_____ in 2020-21 to attend college."

3. They can write letters of recommendation.

4. They can help you select the best scholarship opportunities from among the many options.

5. They can make introductions to key people.

6. They can review your letters of inquiry, applications, etc.

7. They can serve as your accountability team to whom you will hold yourself accountable for completing the five steps outlined in this book.

In fact, it is helpful for each Support Team member to get their own copies of this book so that everyone can follow along as a group and literally get on the same page!

Size

What's the best number of people to have on your Support Team?

You should have at least 3 people and no more than 8-10. Fewer than 3 will make it difficult to gain momentum and won't give you the range of perspective that you need. More than 10 makes the group unwieldy and challenging to manage.

CollegeScholarships.me

- **ACTION**: If you have trouble or would like help in creating your own unique Support Team, visit CollegeScholarships.me.

- **ACTION**: For more info on supportive and hindering roles of a Support Team, visit Appendix F.

Chapter 2

STEP 2 - Create Your Budget of Expenses

According to CNBC[13], "It costs $74,570 a year to go to Stanford."

You may not want to or plan to attend Stanford University. So, how much do you think it will cost you to attend and complete college?

Before we begin to find scholarships and begin applying (chapter 4), in Chapter 2, we'll explore how to estimate your costs to attend college in 2020-21 (July 1, 2020 through June 30, 2021).

So, your budget estimate of expenses should start July 1, 2020 and end June 30, 2021. This 12-month period is called the "academic fiscal year 2020-21." It is the academic fiscal year followed by most colleges and universities.

On the other hand, the U.S. federal government uses a different "federal fiscal year 2020-21" that starts October 1, 2020, and ends September 30, 2021. But, don't worry

---

[13] www.cnbc.com/2019/04/26/it-costs-74570-to-go-to-stanford-but-heres-how-much-students-pay.html

about that. Focus instead on the "academic fiscal year 2020-21."

Of course, if instead of a 4-year bachelor degree, you wish to attain a certificate of completion, 2-year associate degree, 2-year graduate degree, or other degree, the amount will be different. But, the process of creating a budget (step 1) is the same. Create your budget of expenses, first!

An Average Yearly Cost Estimate For A Full-Time Undergraduate Student

To help you get started, here is a general overview of core expenses at public and private schools...

	2 Year Community College	Public Four Year In State	Public Four Year Out of State	Private Non-Profit 4 Year	Private For Profit	Trade School
Books and Supplies	$1,390	$1,250	$1,250	$1,230	$1,200	1,100
Personal Expenses	$2,270	$2,110	$2,110	$1,650	$1,650	$2,200
Housing & Food	N/A	$10,440	$10,440	$11,890	$13,310	N/A
Transportation to School and/or Work	$1,760	$1,160	$1,160	$1,070	$1,070	$1,850

Tuition and Fees	$3,520	$9,650	$24,930	$33,480	$16,000	$9,850
Totals	$8,090	$24,610	$39,880	$49,320	$33,230	$15,000

The table above is meant to be a "starting place" for you to begin estimating your college costs. It is helpful to do a "more accurate estimate breakdown for all of your expenses" once you've identified a school that you would like to attend. Tuition and fees vary from college to college.

The more accurate and relevant your budget for expenses can be, the easier it will be for you to begin to find scholarships that will cover your college costs. You want to be able to ultimately say to your Support Team and other people, "I need $_____ in 2020-21 to attend college."

Most colleges have financial aid administrators and officers who can help you calculate your costs at their institutions. Check with your financial aid office for tuition costs specific to your college.

Here is a resource from the U.S. Department of education, as well as several college budget calculator resources and info on tax benefits to parents...

RESOURCE

- studentaid.ed.gov/sa/prepare-for-college/budgeting/creating-your-budget

College Budget Calculator

Resources

1. studentloans.gov/myDirectLoan/counselingInstru ctions.action

2. mappingyourfuture.org/money/budgetcalculator.c fm

3. finaid.org/calculators/studentbudget.phtml

Bonus: Tax Benefits to Parents

Feel free to share this tax benefit information with your parents! According to the U.S. Department of Education[14], "parents (should) read *IRS Publication 970, Tax Benefits for Education*[15] to see which federal income tax benefits might apply to your situation. Here are some highlights:

- Tax Credits for Higher Education Expenses[16]

- Coverdell Education Savings Account[17]

---

[14]14 studentaid.ed.gov/sa/types/tax-benefits#qualified-tuition-programs

[15] www.irs.gov/pub/irs-pdf/p970.pdf

[16] studentaid.ed.gov/sa/types/tax-benefits#credits

[17] studentaid.ed.gov/sa/types/tax-benefits#cloverdell-account

- Qualified Tuition Programs (QTPs; also known as 529 Plans)[18]

- Student Loan Interest Deduction[19]

- Using IRA Withdrawals for College Costs[20]

Two tax credits help offset the costs (tuition, fees, books, supplies, equipment) of college or career school by reducing the amount of your income tax:

- The American Opportunity Credit[21] allows you to claim up to $2,500 per student per year for the first four years of school as the student works toward a degree or similar credential.

- The Lifetime Learning Credit[22] allows you to claim up to $2,000 per student per year for any college or career school tuition and fees, as well as for books, supplies, and equipment that were required for the course and had to be purchased from the school."

---

[18] studentaid.ed.gov/sa/types/tax-benefits#529-plans

[19] studentaid.ed.gov/sa/types/tax-benefits#interest-deduction

[20] studentaid.ed.gov/sa/types/tax-benefits#ira-withdrawals

[21] irs.gov/publications/p970#en_US_2017_publink100077522

[22] irs.gov/publications/p970#en_US_2017_publink100076820

Parents should check with their accountants to make sure they're taking advantage of any higher education tax credit.

- **ACTION** - Check with your financial aid office for tuition costs specific to your college.

- **ACTION** - Calculate your list of expenses to attend college for FY 2020-21.

- **ACTION** - Declare to your Support Team and other people, "I need $_____ in 2020-21 to attend college."

Chapter 3

STEP 3 - Complete Your FAFSA®

According to the U.S. Department of Education[23], "there are three primary types of federal student aid:

1. Grants—financial aid that doesn't have to be repaid (unless, for example, you withdraw from school and owe a refund)

2. Work-study—a work program through which you earn money to help you pay for school

3. Loans—borrowed money for college or career school; you must repay your loans, with interest"

Of course, we only recommend #1 (grants… or scholarships) and #2 (work study) because they do not have to be paid back!

Regardless of any additional college scholarships to which you will apply, before you begin to apply to various scholarship providers featured in this book, Chapter 3 invites you to take action on Step 3… **complete your Free Application for Federal Student Aid (FAFSA®)**…

studentaid.ed.gov/sa/fafsa

---

[23] studentaid.ed.gov/sa/fafsa

The 2020–21 FAFSA® form became available on Oct. 1, 2019, for the 2020–21 award year (which runs from July 1, 2020, to June 30, 2021)...

FAFSA® Form 2020-21[24] (July 1, 2020 - June 30, 2021)

According to the U.S. Department of Education[25], there are three important FAFSA® deadlines to consider…

2020–21 FAFSA® Deadlines

- **"Federal Deadline** - Online applications must be submitted by 11:59 p.m. Central time (CT) on June 30, 2021. Any corrections or updates must be submitted by 11:59 p.m. CT on Sept. 11, 2021.

- **College Deadlines** - Each college or career school might have its own deadline. Check with the schools you're interested in attending. You might also want to ask your school about its definition of an application deadline, whether it is the date the school receives your FAFSA form or the date your FAFSA form is processed.

- **State Deadlines** - Each state has its own deadline."

2020–21 State Deadlines

---

[24] studentaid.ed.gov/sa/fafsa
[25] studentaid.ed.gov/sa/fafsa/deadlines

According to the U.S. Department of Education[26], here are the deadlines for states, provinces and territories deadlines for applying…

State	Deadline
Alabama	Check with your financial aid administrator.
Alaska	Alaska Education Grant: As soon as possible after Oct. 1, 2019. Awards are made until funds are depleted.
	Alaska Performance Scholarship: For priority consideration, submit your application by June 30, 2020. Awards are made until funds are depleted.
Alberta	Contact your financial aid office. There is no state (or province) deadline for Alberta.
American Samoa	Check with your financial aid administrator. Additional forms might be required.
Arizona	Check with your financial aid administrator.

---

[26] studentaid.ed.gov/sa/fafsa/deadlines

Arkansas	Academic Challenge: June 1, 2020, by midnight CT.
	Higher Education Opportunity Grant: June 1, 2020, by midnight CT.
	Workforce Grant: Check with your financial aid administrator.
British Columbia	Contact your financial aid office. There is no state (or province) deadline for British Columbia.
California	For many state financial aid programs: March 2, 2020 (date postmarked).
	Cal Grant also requires submission of a school-certified GPA by March 2, 2020.
	Applicants are encouraged to obtain proof of mailing their GPA and to retain a copy of their GPA form.
	For additional community college Cal Grants: Sept. 2, 2020 (date postmarked).
	If you're a noncitizen without a Social Security card or had one issued through the federal Deferred Action for Childhood Arrivals program, you should fill out the California Dream Act Application found at caldreamact.org. You don't need to fill out a FAFSA form to be eligible for California student financial aid. Contact the California Student Aid Commission (csac.ca.gov) or your financial aid

administrator for more information. Additional forms might be required. Applicants are encouraged to keep a record of their submission by printing out their online FAFSA confirmation page or obtaining proof of mailing the FAFSA form.

Canada	Contact your financial aid office. There is no state (or province) deadline for Canada.
Colorado	Check with your financial aid administrator.
Connecticut	For priority consideration, submit your application by midnight CT, Feb. 15, 2020. Additional forms might be required. Contact your financial aid administrator or your state agency.
Delaware	April 15, 2020, by midnight CT.
District of Columbia	For priority consideration, submit your FAFSA form by May 1, 2020. For the DC Tuition Assistance Grant (DCTAG), complete the DC OneApp and submit supporting documents by May 31, 2020, to be given priority consideration.
Federated States of Micronesia	Check with your financial aid administrator. Additional forms might be required.

Florida	May 15, 2020 (date processed).
Foreign Country	Contact your financial aid office. There is no state deadline for foreign countries.
Georgia	Check with your financial aid administrator.
Guam	Check with your financial aid administrator. Additional forms might be required.
Hawaii	Check with your financial aid administrator. Additional forms might be required.
Idaho	Opportunity Grant: For priority consideration, submit your application by midnight CT, March 1, 2020. Additional forms might be required. Contact your financial aid administrator or your state agency.
Illinois	As soon as possible after Oct. 1, 2019. Visit isac.org for Monetary Award Program renewal deadline information. Awards are made until funds are depleted.

Indiana	Adult Student Grant: As soon as possible after Oct. 1, 2019. Awards are made until funds are depleted. New applicants must submit additional forms at ScholarTrack.IN.gov.
	Workforce Ready Grant: As soon as possible after Oct. 1, 2019.
	Frank O'Bannon Grant: April 15, 2020, by midnight CT.
	21st Century Scholarship: April 15, 2020, by midnight CT.
Iowa	July 1, 2020, by midnight CT. Earlier priority deadlines might exist for certain programs. Additional forms might be required.
Kansas	For priority consideration, submit your application by midnight CT, April 1, 2020. Additional forms might be required. Contact your financial aid administrator or your state agency.
Kentucky	As soon as possible after Oct. 1, 2019. Awards are made until funds are depleted.
Louisiana	July 1, 2021 (July 1, 2020 recommended).

Maine	May 1, 2020, by midnight CT.
Manitoba	Contact your financial aid office. There is no state (or province) deadline for Manitoba.
Marshall Islands	Check with your financial aid administrator. Additional forms might be required.
Maryland	March 1, 2020, by midnight CT.
Massachusetts	For priority consideration, submit your application by midnight CT, May 1, 2020.
Mexico	Contact your financial aid office. There is no state deadline for Mexico.
Michigan	March 1, 2020, by midnight CT.
Minnesota	30 days after term starts, by midnight CT.
Mississippi	June 1, 2020, by midnight CT.
Missouri	For priority consideration, submit your application by Feb. 3, 2020. Applications are accepted through April 1, 2020, at midnight CT.
Montana	For priority consideration, submit your application by Dec. 1, 2019. Check with your financial aid administrator. Additional

forms might be required.

Nebraska	Check with your financial aid administrator.
Nevada	Silver State Opportunity Grant: As soon as possible after Oct. 1, 2019. Awards are made until funds are depleted.
	Nevada Promise Scholarship: April 1, 2020. Additional forms might be required. Awards are made until funds are depleted.
	All other aid: Check with your financial aid administrator. Additional forms might be required.
New Brunswick	Contact your financial aid office. There is no state (or province) deadline for New Brunswick.
New Hampshire	Check with your financial aid administrator. Additional forms might be required.
New Jersey	2019–20 Tuition Aid Grant recipients: April 15, 2020, by midnight CT.
	All other applicants: Fall and spring terms: Sept. 15, 2020, by midnight CT.
	All other applicants: Spring term only: Feb.

15, 2021, by midnight CT.

New Mexico	Check with your financial aid administrator.
New York	June 30, 2021, by midnight CT. Additional forms might be required.
Newfoundland	Contact your financial aid office. There is no state (or province) deadline for Newfoundland.
Newfoundland/ Labrador	Contact your financial aid office. There is no state (or province) deadline for Newfoundland/Labrador.
North Carolina	As soon as possible after Oct. 1, 2019. Awards are made until funds are depleted.
North Dakota	As soon as possible after Oct. 1, 2019. Awards are made until funds are depleted.
N. Mariana Islands	For priority consideration, submit your application by midnight CT, April 30, 2020. Additional forms might be required.
Northwest Territories	Contact your financial aid office. There is no state (or province) deadline for Northwest Territories.

Nova Scotia	Contact your financial aid office. There is no state (or province) deadline for Nova Scotia.
Nunavut	Contact your financial aid office. There is no state (or province) deadline for Nunavut.
Ohio	Oct. 1, 2020, by midnight CT.
Oklahoma	As soon as possible after Oct. 1, 2019. Awards are made until funds are depleted.
Ontario	Contact your financial aid office. There is no state (or province) deadline for Ontario.
Oregon	Oregon Opportunity Grant: As soon as possible after Oct. 1, 2019. Awards are made until funds are depleted.
	OSAC Private Scholarships: March 1, 2020. Additional forms might be required.
	Oregon Promise Grant: Contact your state agency. Additional forms might be required.
Palau	Check with your financial aid administrator. Additional forms might be required.

Pennsylvania	All first-time applicants enrolled in a community college, business, trade, or technical school, hospital school of nursing, designated Pennsylvania Open-Admission institution, or nontransferable two-year program: Aug. 1, 2020, by midnight CT.
	All other applicants: May 1, 2020, by midnight CT. Additional forms might be required.
Prince Edward Island	Contact your financial aid office. There is no state (or province) deadline for Prince Edward Island.
Puerto Rico	Check with your financial aid administrator.
Quebec (PQ)	Contact your financial aid office. There is no state (or province) deadline for Quebec (PQ).
Quebec (QC)	Contact your financial aid office. There is no state (or province) deadline for Quebec (QC).
Rhode Island	Check with your financial aid administrator. Additional forms might be required.
Saskatchewan	Contact your financial aid office. There is no state (or province) deadline for Saskatchewan.

South Carolina	SC Commission on Higher Education Need-based Grants: As soon as possible after Oct. 1, 2019. Awards are made until funds are depleted.
	Tuition Grants: June 30, 2020, by midnight CT.
South Dakota	Check with your financial aid administrator. Additional forms might be required.
Tennessee	State Grant: Prior-year recipients receive award if eligible and apply by Feb. 1, 2020.
	All other awards made to neediest applicants. Awards are made until funds are depleted.
	Tennessee Promise: Feb. 1, 2020 (date received).
	State Lottery: Fall term: Sept. 1, 2020 (date received).
	State Lottery: Spring and summer terms: Feb. 1, 2021 (date received).
Texas	For priority consideration, submit your application by Jan. 15, 2020. Additional forms might be required. Private and two-year institutions might have different deadlines. Check with your financial aid

administrator.

U.S. Virgin Islands	Check with your financial aid administrator. Additional forms might be required.
Utah	Check with your financial aid administrator. Awards are made until funds are depleted. Additional forms might be required.
Vermont	As soon as possible after Oct. 1, 2019. Awards are made until funds are depleted. Additional forms might be required.
Virginia	Check with your financial aid administrator. Additional forms might be required.
Washington	As soon as possible after Oct. 1, 2019. Awards are made until funds are depleted. Students ineligible for federal aid but who meet state financial aid program and residency requirements should complete the Washington Application for State Financial Aid at readysetgrad.org/wasfa instead of the FAFSA form. Contact the Washington Student Achievement Council (readysetgrad.org/wasfa) or your financial aid administrator for more information.

West Virginia	PROMISE Scholarship: March 1, 2020. New applicants must submit additional forms at cfwv.com. Contact your financial aid administrator or your state agency.
	WV Higher Education Grant Program: April 15, 2020.
Wisconsin	Check with your financial aid administrator.
Wyoming	Check with your financial aid administrator. Additional forms might be required.
Yukon	Contact your financial aid office. There is no state deadline (or province) for Yukon.

Federal Pell Grants

According to the U.S. Department of Education[27], "Federal Pell Grants usually are awarded only to undergraduate students who display exceptional financial need and have not earned a bachelor's, graduate, or professional degree. (In some cases, however, a student enrolled in a postbaccalaureate teacher certification program might receive a Federal Pell Grant.)

---

[27] studentaid.ed.gov/sa/fafsa/deadlines

You will have to fill out the FAFSA® form every year you're in school in order to stay eligible for federal student aid."

How Much Can You Expect from Your Pell Grant?

According to the U.S. Department of Education[28], "Amounts can change yearly. The maximum Federal Pell Grant award is $6,195 for the 2019–20 award year (July 1, 2019, to June 30, 2020)."

According to the Nation College Access Network[29], "Congress is still debating what the federal spending levels will be for fiscal year 2020... Because of the way the federal fiscal year overlaps with the academic award year, the dollar amounts lawmakers are currently debating will set the Pell Grant program funding for the 2020-21 year

The good news is that, most likely, the Pell Grant maximum will be at least the current $6,195. The House appropriations subcommittee on Labor, Health and Human Services, and Education passed funding levels that would allow for a $150 increase, to a maximum of $6,345. Their Senate counterparts were rumored to be working in September on a bill that included a $135 increase."

---

[28] studentaid.ed.gov/sa/types/grants-scholarships/pell
[29] collegeaccess.org/news/478470/What-is-the-2020-21-Pell-Grant-Max-Award.htm

U.S. Department of Education[30] adds, "The amount you get, though, will depend on

- your Expected Family Contribution,[31]

- the cost of attendance (determined by your school for your specific program),

- your status as a full-time or part-time student, and

- your plans to attend school for a full academic year or less."

The U.S. Department of Education[32] says that your Expected Family Contribution (EFC) is "an index number that college financial aid staff use to determine how much financial aid you would receive if you were to attend their school. The information you report on your FAFSA® form is used to calculate your EFC.

The EFC is calculated according to a formula established by law. Your family's taxed and untaxed income, assets, and benefits (such as unemployment or Social Security) all could be considered in the formula. Also considered are your family size and the number of family members who will attend college or career school during the year.

---

[30] studentaid.ed.gov/sa/types/grants-scholarships/pell

[31] studentaid.ed.gov/sa/fafsa/next-steps/how-calculated#efc

[32] studentaid.ed.gov/sa/fafsa/next-steps/how-calculated#efc

The EFC Formula[33] guide shows exactly how an EFC is calculated."

Help with FAFSA®

The College Parents Association suggests 8 steps for filing your FAFSA®...

  collegeparents.org/2013/02/19/8-steps-filing-your-fafsa

The National Association of Student Financial Aid Administrators (NASFAA) provides these FAFSA® Tips and Common Mistakes to Avoid...

  nasfaa.org/fafsa_tips

- **ACTION** - File your FAFSA®.

33

  studentaid.ed.gov/sa/resources#efc

Chapter 4

STEP 4 - Find & Apply (Top 10 Places to Find Scholarships)

According to the Federal Student Aid Office[34] of the U.S. Department of Education, "try these free sources of information about scholarships:

- the financial aid office at a college or career school

- a high school or TRIO counselor

- the U.S. Department of Labor's FREE scholarship search tool[35]

- federal agencies[36]

- your state grant agency[37]

- your library's reference section

- foundations, religious or community organizations, local businesses, or civic groups

---

[34] studentaid.ed.gov/sa/types/grants-scholarships/finding-scholarships
[35] careeronestop.org/toolkit/training/find-scholarships.aspx
[36] studentaid.ed.gov/sa/types#federal-aid
[37] www2.ed.gov/about/contacts/state/index.html

- organizations (including professional associations) related to your field of interest

- ethnicity-based organizations

- your employer or your parents' employers"

Let's take a look at the top 10 places to find and apply for scholarships in 2020! Some of the free sources listed above are included here...

Place #1 - Federal Government

Here are four resources to help you understand unique opportunities for federal grants and scholarships:

- studentaid.ed.gov/sa/sites/default/files/federal-grant-programs.pdf

- studentaid.ed.gov/sa/types#federal-aid

- wemakescholars.com/government/us-federal-government/scholarships

- bu.edu/wll/files/2013/05/Scholarships-for-students.pdf

The U.S. Department of Education[38] recommends this information regarding discretionary (or "competitive") grants and scholarships...

---

[38] www2.ed.gov/fund/grants-apply.html?src=pn

"Eligibility and Forecasts

- **Find Grant Programs by Eligibility**[39]: who can apply for what

- **ED grants forecast**[40]: competitions opening soon

Application Information

- *Federal Register* **Notices**[41]: competitions and other announcements

- **Apply**[42]: Deadlines, amounts, applications, more

- **Forms**[43]

Online Applications

- **Grants.gov:**[44] Application packages for ED programs

- **G5**[45]: Application packages on ED's online grants system

---

[39] studentaid.ed.gov/sa/sites/default/files/federal-grant-programs.pdf

[40] www2.ed.gov/fund/grant/find/edlite-forecast.html

[41] federalregister.gov/articles/search?conditions%5Bagency_ids%5D=126&conditions%5Btype%5D=NOTICE

[42] www2.ed.gov/fund/grant/apply/grantapps/index.html

[43] www2.ed.gov/fund/grant/apply/appforms/appforms.html

[44] www.grants.gov/search-grants.html?agencyCode=ED

[45] www.g5.gov/int/wps/portal

Other grant information

- **IES funding**[46]**:** funding opportunities from ED's Institute for Education Sciences

- **Grants.gov:** federal government grant competitions

- **All formula grants**[47]

- **A-Z list of all programs**[48]

- **Grantmaking at ED**[49]**:** a summary of ED's discretionary grant process

- **Risk Management Tools**[50]

- **Requesting Reconsideration of Denial of Continuation Award**[51]

- **More information about ED programs**[52]"

U.S. Department of Labor's Scholarship Finder

- careeronestop.org/toolkit/training/find-scholarships.aspx

---

[46] ies.ed.gov/funding
[47] ed.gov (search for "formula grants")
[48] ed.gov (search for "scholarship programs")
[49] www2.ed.gov/fund/grant/about/grantmaking/index.html
[50] www2.ed.gov/fund/grant/about/risk-management-tools.html?src=grants-page
[51] www2.ed.gov/fund/grant/about/requesting-reconsideration.html?src=grants-page
[52] www2.ed.gov/programs/?src=apply-page

Federal Work Study

Federal Work Study (FWS) is a national program that allows you to work (at or above minimum wage) in which you do not have to pay the money back. However, you have to work for it. According to Federal Student Aid[53], an office of the U.S. Department of Education, "research has shown that students who work part-time jobs manage their time better than those who don't!"

According the U.S. Department of Education[54], Federal Work Study (FWS) "provides funds for part-time employment to help needy students to finance the costs of postsecondary education. Students can receive FWS funds at approximately 3,400 participating postsecondary institutions. Hourly wages must not be less than the federal minimum wage.

A participating institution applies each year for FWS funding by submitting a Fiscal Operations Report and Application to Participate (FISAP) to the U.S. Department of Education. Using a statutory formula, the Department allocates funds based on the institution's previous funding level and the aggregate need of eligible students in attendance in the prior year.

In most cases, the school or the employer must pay up to a 50 percent share of a student's wages under FWS. (In some cases, such as FWS jobs as reading or mathematics tutors,

---

[53] studentaid.ed.gov/sa/fafsa/next-steps/accept-aid
[54] www2.ed.gov/programs/fws/index.html

the federal share of the wages can be as high as 100 percent.)

Students may be employed by: the institution itself; a federal, state, or local public agency; a private nonprofit organization; or a private for-profit organization. Institutions must use at least 7 percent of their Work-Study allocation to support students working in community service jobs, including: reading tutors for preschool age or elementary school children; mathematics tutors for students enrolled in elementary school through ninth grade; literacy tutors in a family literacy project performing family literacy activities; or emergency preparedness and response.

Students must file a *Free Application for Federal Student Aid (FAFSA)* as part of the application process for FWS assistance. The FAFSA can be completed on the Web at http://www.fafsa.ed.gov. For more information on the student aid award process, see the Federal Pell Grant Program (# 84.063, also under topical heading Federal Student Aid)."

Summary

The National Association of Student Financial Aid Administrators (NASFAA) provides this Federal Student Aid Program Summary for 2020-21...

- studentaid.ed.gov/sa/sites/default/files/2020-21-fafsa.pdf?_ga=2.247171075.660913828.156981979 5-742414768.1564442400

- **ACTION** - After you file your FAFSA®, start **looking for a work-study job on-campus and off-campus**. Contact the financial aid office or career center on campus. Keep in mind that your college has a limited amount of work-study funds or positions. Be pro-active and find a work-study job as soon as you can. Also, since institutions are required to use at least 7 percent of their work-study funds for community service jobs off-campus, look for these opportunities, as well.

- **BENEFIT** - According to the U.S. Department of Education[55], "One of the benefits of earning income through a Federal Work-Study position is that those earnings do not count against you when you complete the FAFSA form. There's a question on the FAFSA form that asks how much was earned through work-study during a particular tax year; make sure to answer that question accurately (next year) so the amount can be factored out. If you do not know how much you earned, you can contact the financial aid office at your school for help."

---

[55] blog.ed.gov/2017/07/8-things-you-should-know-about-federal-work-study/

Place #2 - State Government

The U.S. Department of Education[56] suggests that "Even if you're not eligible for federal aid, you might be eligible for financial aid from your state. Contact your state grant agency for more information."

Here is a link for you to use to contact the department of education, the higher education agency, special education agency and adult education agency in your state (commonwealth and territory)...

- www2.ed.gov/about/contacts/state/index.html

Example: State of California

For example, when I follow the link above to search for resources within the state of California, here are the contacts and resources that appear...

State Department of Education

California Department of Education

1430 N Street

Sacramento, CA 95814-5901

Phone: (916) 319-0800

Fax: (916) 319-0100

Website: **cde.ca.gov**

---

[56] studentaid.ed.gov/sa/types

State Higher Education Agency

California Student Aid Commission

P.O. Box 419027

Rancho Cordova, CA 95741-9027

Toll-Free: (888) 224-7268

Fax: (916) 526-8004

Website: **csac.ca.gov**

Special Education Agency

Special Education Division

California State Department of Education

Suite 2401

1430 N Street

Sacramento, CA 95814-5901

Phone: (916) 445-4613

Fax: (916) 327-3706

Website: **cde.ca.gov/sp/se**

State Adult Education Agency

Adult Education

Career and College Transition Division

1430 N Street, Suite 4202

Sacramento, CA 95814

Phone: (916) 445-2652

Fax: (916) 327-7089

Website: **cde.ca.gov/re/di/or/scald.asp**

According to the National Association of Student Financial Aid Administrators[57], "Almost every state education agency has at least one grant or scholarship available to residents, and many have a long list of student aid programs. Eligibility is usually restricted to state residents attending a college in-state, but that's not always the case. There are annual deadlines for most programs (if you miss a deadline, be sure to try again next year). Select your state to find out what financial aid programs may be available to you through your state education agency. Also check out state and regional tuition exchanges and keep in mind that other state-sponsored aid may available through non-profit organizations in your area..."

---

[57] www.nasfaa.org/State_Financial_Aid_Programs

- nasfaa.org/State_Financial_Aid_Programs – Go to the website URL. Click on your state to check out the financial programs in your state…

State & Regional College Tuition Discounts

According to the National Association of Student Financial Aid Administrators[58], "Many states have programs that allow residents to attend university in another state, without having to pay out-of-state tuition. Check with your state, or with universities that you're interested in, about available tuition exchange or reciprocity programs, and ask about how to sign up. The FAFSA is not required for these programs, generally."

---

[58] www.nasfaa.org/State_Regional_Tuition_Exchanges

- **ACTION** - Check with the department of education, the higher education agency, special education agency and adult education agency in your state (commonwealth and territory)... www2.ed.gov/about/contacts/state/index.html

- **ACTION** - Check out the financial programs in your state... nasfaa.org/State_Financial_Aid_Programs

Place #3 - Websites

Here are 12 top websites with free databases to assist you with your search for scholarships:

1. AdventuresInEducation.org

2. Chegg.com

3. CollegeBoard.com

4. CollegeExpress.com

5. CollegeNet.com

6. CollegeScholarships.org

7. FastWeb.com

8. moolahSPOT.com

9. SallieMae.com/scholarships

10. Scholarships.com

11. StudentScholarshipSearch.com

12. SuperCollege.com

- **ACTION** - Check out the 12 websites above.

Place #4 - Civic Organizations

According to GuideStar.org (codes Y40, Y41 and Y42), there are 36,289 civic, fraternal, service and professional organizations operating in the U.S. such as Knights of Columbus, Lions Clubs International, Masons, NAACP, National Civic League, National Council of Jewish Women, Rotary International, Shriners, local chapters, etc.

According to Financial Aid Finder[59], "joining a service association like the Rotary Club, Circle K, Key Club or Jaycees as a student can be a great way to meet people and participate in community events, while making the world a better place.

You may not know that there are also scholarships available to members of service organizations. Like many other membership organizations, these organizations not only value public service, but also want to see their members be successful in their higher education pursuits.

---

[59] financialaidfinder.com/student-scholarship-search/association-sponsored-scholarships/civic-organization-scholarships/

51

Of course, they also understand that the rising cost of college tuition makes scholarships and other financial aid necessary for most students to obtain a college degree.

While most young people are not members of Kiwanis International themselves, most schools have chapters of Circle K, the college and university program of Kiwanis and high schools have Key Club, another Kiwanis program. Each district of Circle K offers one $1,000 scholarship to a member each year. This is in addition to merit-based scholarships for Circle K members that are distributed every year at the Kiwanis International Conference.

Rotary International also offers financial aid for members (or potential members) in the form of a need-based scholarship funding pool.

There are also many scholarships for members of Junior Chamber International or its JAYCEES program. Seeking to promote leadership and civic responsibility, the Jaycees Charles R. Ford for active members rewards high academic achievement and proven leadership skills. Individual Jaycees chapters are an even greater source of money for college, and checking in with your local chapter is your best bet for getting a Jaycees scholarship for college."

- **ACTION** - Identify the civic organizations (with assets and revenue) around your residence and/or school of choice by visiting GuideStar.org (use cause areas or NTEE codes Y40, Y41 and Y42).

- **ACTION** - Write letters of inquiry to civic organizations you identified.

Place #5 - Churches

Many churches and religious groups offer scholarships. Check with your local church office staff.

For Christian students, here are 25 great scholarship opportunities from Top Ten Online Colleges[60] from Baptist, Catholic, Church of Christ, Lutheran, Methodist, Mormon, Presbyterian, Quakers, Roman Catholic, United Church of Christ denominations:

1. Allen Chapel African Methodist Episcopal Church Scholarship (Deadline: May 1)

2. Baptist Life Scholarships (Deadline: May 31)

3. Cannon Endowment Scholarship (Deadline: April 1)

4. Catholic Knights College Scholarship (Deadline: March 31)

5. Chris Hernandez Memorial Scholarship (Deadline: April 27)

6. Clare Boothe Luce Program (Deadline: March 14)

7. Diamonds in the Rough Ministry International Scholarship (Deadline: April 20)

---

[60] top10onlinecolleges.org/scholarships-for/christian-students

8. Faith & Education Scholarship (Deadline: April 12)

9. Foundation for College Christian Leaders Scholarships (Deadline: May 22)

10. Hanson Quaker Leadership Scholarship (Deadline: Varies each year)

11. Ed E. Gladys Hurly Foundation Scholarship (Deadline: June 30)

12. Herbert W. & Corinne Chilstrom Scholarship (Deadline: February 15)

13. Italian Catholic Federation Scholarships (Deadline: March 15)

14. Lett Scholarship Fund (Deadline: January 31)

15. Lydia Scholarship (Deadline: March 1)

16. Make a Difference! Seminarian Scholarship (Deadline: Varies)

17. Mormon Tabernacle Choir Scholarships (Deadline: Varies)

18. Nairobi Pentecostal Bible College (NPBC) Scholarship (Deadline: July 1 for Fall)

19. Mary Hill Davis Ethnic/Minority Student Scholarship Program (Deadline: April 15)

20. National Presbyterian College Scholarship (Deadline: March 1)

21. Oakwood University Premier Scholarship (Deadline: Varies)

22. Reverend Ray Ley Scholarship Fund (Deadline: Varies)

23. The Winston-Salem Foundation Emma Kapp Ogburn Memorial Fund (Deadline: June 15)

24. YCL Young Christian Leaders Scholarship (Deadline: 15th of each month)

25. WMU Foundation Scholarships (Deadline: Varies)

- **ACTION** - Schedule a meeting with the office staff of your church.

- **ACTION** - Check out the 25 great scholarship opportunities from Top Ten Online Colleges[61] listed above.

Place #6 - Nonprofit Organizations

According to the U.S. Department of Education, "Many organizations offer scholarships or grants to help students pay for college or career school. This free money can make a real difference in how affordable your education is."

---

[61] top10onlinecolleges.org/scholarships-for/christian-students

According to GuideStar.org, there are 25,201 charitable nonprofits in the U.S. that are able to offer some form of scholarships and financial aid.

Unfortunately, only 41% of these (10,325) have enough assets and annual revenue to approach. These (with assets and annual revenue) are the ones you want to approach! For example, in California, there are 975 nonprofit agencies with assets/revenue to be approached for scholarships. Once you've identified the nonprofits around where you live AND where you plan to attend college (visit GuideStar.org and search for "cause area" B82), you might consider mailing a letter of interest.

- **ACTION** - Identify the nonprofit organizations (with assets and revenue) around your residence and school of choice by visiting GuideStar.org (use "cause area," "sub-cause area" or "NTEE code" B82 - Scholarships & Student Financial Aid).

- **ACTION** - Write letters of inquiry to nonprofit organizations you identified.

Place #7 - Employers (Yours & Your Parents', Too!)

Check with your employer and the employer for your parents. Ask employers if they provide scholarships for their employees (or children of their employees).

According to Top 10 Online Colleges[62], "Corporate scholarships offer big bucks in mass quantities for young consumers who are pursuing their own 'American Dream' in college.

Searching through the Fortune 500 list, you'll find numerous companies who have created charitable arms to donate millions. Whether they're in retail, healthcare, telecommunications, or manufacturing, profitable corporations increasingly turn revenue into philanthropy for education. In fact, NPT reported that corporate giving increased by 3.9 percent to $18.46 billion from 2014 to 2015. Multinational companies typically choose a higher number of recipients than smaller community foundations, but competition can be strong with an extended pool of hopefuls."

Here are 25 corporations that offer scholarships along with their scholarship deadlines (source: Top 10 Online Colleges[63]):

1. AXA Achievement Scholarship (deadline: December 15)

2. BP Community Scholarship Program(deadline: March 24)

3. Bristol-Myers Squibb Scholarship (deadline: March 31)

---

[62] top10onlinecolleges.org/scholarships-for/corporate-scholarships/
[63] Ibid.

4. Chevron Corporation Scholarship (deadline: May 1)

5. Coca-Cola Leaders of Promise Scholarships (deadline: May 2)

6. CVS Pharmacy, Inc. Business Scholarships (deadline: March 31)

7. Dell Scholars Program Scholarship (deadline: January 15)

8. Delta Air Lines Engineering Scholarship (deadline: November 14)

9. ExxonMobil/LNESC National Scholarship (deadline: April 15)

10. Foot Locker Athletes Scholarships (deadline: April 15)

11. Ford Driving Dreams Scholarships (deadline: March 14)

12. GE-Reagan Foundation Scholarship (deadline: January 5)

13. Google Lime Scholarship Program (deadline: December 4)

14. John Deere Dealer Scholarships (deadline: February 8)

15. Lockheed Martin Corporation Scholarships (deadline: February 15)

16. Marriott International Scholarships (deadline: January 13)

17. Nordson Corporation BUILDS Scholarships (deadline: May 15)

18. Panera Best of the Batch Scholarships (deadline: April 14)

19. Raytheon-SVA Patriot Scholarships (deadline: March 31)

20. Shell Oil Company Technical Scholarships (deadline: March 2)

21. State Farm Good Neighbor Scholarships (deadline: March 1)

22. TMCF MillerCoors Scholarship Program (deadline: April 30)

23. Toshiba Machine Co. Scholarship (deadline: February 28)

24. Tylenol Future Care Scholarships (deadline: June 30)

25. Walmart Associate Scholarship (deadline: March 1)

For example, Walmart "employees can receive up to $2,000 for associate, $3,000 bachelor's, or $2,000 for graduate programs each year." (source: Top 10 Online Colleges[64])

---

[64] www.top10onlinecolleges.org/scholarships-for/corporate-scholarships

According to Scholarships.com, here are 113 employer scholarships:

A&W

Abbott Laboratories

Adobe Systems

ADP

Aetna

Airline Employee

Alcoa

Amazon.com

American Airlines

American Cancer Society

AT&T

Baxter International

Biogen Idec

BMW Group

Bosch

Build A Bear

Burger King

California Grape Grower

California State University Bakersfield

Capital One Financial

Carmax

CenterPoint Energy

Chevron

Chipotle

Chobani

Citigroup

Community Bankers Assoc. of Illinois

ConocoPhillips

Costco

CPS Energy

Cracker Barrel

CVS Pharmacy

Darden Restaurants

DirecTV

Dish Network

Dominion Resources

Duke Energy Corporation

DuPont

Edison International

Emergency Medical Technician (EMT)

Express Scripts

Exxon

Federal Government Employee

Firefighter

Food Service Professional

Footwear & Leather Industry

GameStop

General Electric

General Mills

Genzyme

Golf Caddie

H&R Block, Inc.

Harley Davidson

Hewlett- Packard (HP)

Home Depot

Humana

Hyundai Motors

IBM

Intel

J Crew

JetBlue Airways

Kentucky Fried Chicken

L.L. Bean

Land O' Lakes

Law Enforcement Officer

Long John Silver's

Lowe's

Marathon Petroleum

Mayo Clinic

McDonald's Corporation

Meijer

Morgan Stanley

Mutual of Omaha

National Roofing
Contractors Assoc.

Nordstrom, Inc.

Nucor

Oshkosh

Pacific Gas & Electric

PepsiCo

Pfizer Inc.

Phillips 66

Pizza Hut

Prison Guard

Promotional Products
Industry

Public Service Employee

Rockwell Collins

Roller Skating
Association

SAS

Servco - HI

Southwest Airlines

Starbucks

State Farm

Subway Restaurant

Sunoco

Taco Bell

Texas Instruments

Tj Maxx

Travel Industry

Uline

Union Pacific

United Technologies

US Bank

USDA

Valero Energy

Verizon

Vermont Grocers Assoc.
Member

Wakefield Healthcare
Center

Walgreens

Walmart

Walt Disney	Whole Foods
Wells Fargo	Yum!

- **ACTION** - Schedule a meeting with the Personnel Office of the company where you work.

- **ACTION** - Ask your parent(s) to schedule a meeting with the Personnel Office of the company where he/she works.

Place #8 - Your College Financial Aid Office

According to the U.S. Department of Education[65], "Many schools offer financial aid from their own funds. Find out what might be available to you:

- Visit your school's financial aid page on its website, or ask someone in the financial aid office.

- Ask at the department that offers your course of study; they might have a scholarship for students in your major.

- Fill out any applications the school requires for its own aid, and meet the deadlines."

_____

[65] studentaid.ed.gov/sa/types

According to the National Association of Student Financial Aid Administrators (NASFAA)[66], a Financial Aid Administrator (FAA) is "an individual who works at a college or career school and is responsible for preparing and communicating information on student loans, grants or scholarships, and employment programs. The FAA helps students apply for and receive student aid. The FAA is also capable of analyzing student needs and making professional judgment changes when necessary."

According to the NASFAA[67], "The first mistake many students and families make is assuming they can't afford college. Don't be discouraged by the sticker price of college until you know how much financial aid may be available to you. Financial aid can significantly reduce the cost of college, but it can be tricky to estimate how much student aid you will get. Two factors are generally used to determine who gets student aid and how much they get: need and merit.

- 'Merit-based' aid is given to students who do something exceptionally well (like music, athletics, or academics) or to students who plan to have a career in an area that will benefit the community or the country (like teaching, science, math, and engineering).

---

[66]nasfaa.org/uploads/documents/Award_Notification_Compari son_Worksheet.pdf
[67] www.nasfaa.org/about_financial_aid

- 'Need-based' aid is given to students who demonstrate a lack of financial resources to pay for college.

Some student aid programs use a combination of need and merit to determine eligibility."

- **ACTION** - Schedule a meeting with the financial aid officer or administrator at your college.

Place #9 - Ethnic Groups

According to Ramit Sethi[68], the author of *I Will Teach You to Be Rich*, "ethnic organizations of all stripes tend to offer scholarships. These can help you earn hundreds — if not thousands — in scholarship money.

Many of these are *ethnicity-based*, meaning that you'll have to be a certain race or background in order to qualify for the scholarship.

A few suggestions:

- Asian & Pacific Islander American Scholarship Fund[69]

- The United Negro College Fund[70]

---

[68] iwillteachyoutoberich.com/blog/how-to-get-scholarships
[69] apiasf.org/index.html
[70] scholarships.uncf.org

- The Hispanic Scholarship Fund[71]

- Irish ancestry scholarships[72]

- German ancestry scholarships[73]"

- **ACTION** - Identify the ethnic groups around your residence and school of choice.

- **ACTION** - Write letters of inquiry to ethnic groups you identified.

Place #10 - Hidden Groups & Keys

- **Alumni Groups** -- Many universities have an Alumni Association. According to GuideStar.org, there are 5,125 Alumni Associations at colleges with assets/revenue enough to provide scholarships. Perhaps even more important than scholarship money, Alumni Groups can be great resources for you. They could participate in your ongoing Support Team once you start college! They may even help you find a good work-study job, internship or job during and after college.

---

[71] hsf.net

[72] fastweb.com/directory/scholarships-for-irish-students

[73] fastweb.com/directory/scholarships-for-german-students

- For example, according to the University of Southern California (USC)[74], "The USC Alumni Association and its related entities award nearly $4 million in alumni scholarships to continuing students each year. Individuals must apply for scholarships during the academic year prior to the year of funding. Applicants may apply for multiple scholarships at one time..."

- **Student Clubs** - According to GetSchooled[75], here are 9 clubs that provide scholarships:

  1. *"Black Student Union (BSU)* – Are you in the Black Student Union at your high school? Your involvement with the BSU can earn you college scholarships as early as 9th grade, even if you don't plan to go to college. Syracuse University, Indiana Tech, Loyola University Maryland and 222 other colleges offer up to $5,400 in scholarships for every year of BSU participation. As if that wasn't awesome enough, leadership roles may be eligible for an extra scholarship of up to $3,375 per year according to RaiseMe.

  2. *National Honors Society (NHS)* – The National Honors Society offers exclusive scholarship opportunities to its members. Applications for

---

[74] alumni.usc.edu/alumni-scholarships
[75] getschooled.com/dashboard/article/4081-in-the-mix-badge-9-clubs-orgs-that-lead-to-major-scholarship-money

the 2017-18 school year become available October 6th and will be due January 30th 2018. To be eligible a student must be a high school senior and in good standing with the NHS chapter at their school. (nhs.us/students/the-nhs-scholarship)

3. *Key Club* – If you belong to the Key Club chapter at your school, you might qualify for one of the Key Club International scholarship programs. Applicants must be Key Club members in good standing for at least two years and a graduating senior with a GPA of at last "B" or 3.0 heading to higher education. Each Key Club District determines its own deadlines so you'll need to visit your school's chapter advisor for more information. Key Club is a student-led organization that teaches leadership through community service.

4. *Rotary Club* – The Rotary Foundation and clubs offer its members scholarships for undergraduate and graduate study. The Rotary foundation concentrates on creating sustainable peace, water and health projects with a focus on education, mothers and children, and growing local communities. If you're interested in the Rotary Foundation scholarship program, visit rotary.org/en/our-programs/scholarships.

5. *Speech and Debate Club* – The National Speech and Debate Association is the largest speech

and debate organization in the country and annually gives out major scholarship dollars to debate team members who participate in tournaments! Individual students can't register for the tournament on their own, however, they can definitely incite their schools to help them compete for debate funding for college. Some undergraduate schools with active forensics programs offer scholarships directly to high-achieving high school debate team members. (speechanddebate.org/scholarships)

6. *Lions Club* – The goal of the Lions Club is to make a difference both locally and nationally. One of the ways the organization meets its mission is by providing Lions Club scholarships. A variety of Lions Club scholarships are available through local chapters. The amount of Lions Club scholarships varies based on local guidelines and availability. Students may be required to meet certain eligibility guidelines, including minimum GPAs, submission of essays and submitting letters of recommendation. (temp.lionsclubs.org/EN/pdfs/iad133.pdf)

7. *DECA* – DECA Inc. prepares emerging leaders and entrepreneurs for careers in marketing, finance, hospitality and management in high schools and colleges around the globe. The DECA's scholarship programs offers up to $300,000 annually

through a variety of scholarships exclusive to DECA members. For more information on scholarships offered through DECA, visit deca.org/high-school-programs/scholarships.

8. *NABJ* – The National Association of Black Journalists (NABJ) is the largest organization for journalists of color in the nation, and provides career development as well as educational and other support to its members worldwide. Anyone can join! The NABJ awards scholarships on an annual basis to college and high school members interested in pursuing careers in journalism. Scholarships are worth up to $3,000 a piece. For more information on NABJ scholarships, visit nabj.org/page/seedscholarships.

9. *Robotics Club* – The National Robotics League (NRL) is a manufacturing staff development program of the National Tooling & Machining Association where students design and build remote controlled robots to face-off in a gladiator-style competition. Student teams compete regionally to be able to test their robotic creations and battle for local supremacy. FIRSTInspires.org offers millions of dollars in robotics scholarships to students demonstrating a passion and secure knowledge of robotics engineering. (firstinspires.org/scholarships)"

- National Scholarship Providers Association[76] (546 scholarship providers)

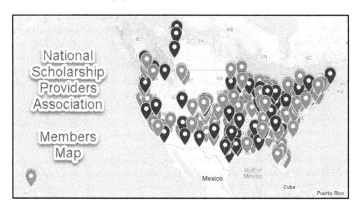

- **ACTION** - Visit GuideStar.org (use cause area or NTEE code B84). Schedule an appointment with the Alumni Group at your school of choice.

- **ACTION** - Check the list of 9 clubs above for any that sound interesting to you.

- **ACTION** - Schedule an appointment with the Student Club at your school of choice.

[76] scholarshipproviders.org/page/MemberMap

- **ACTION** - Identify scholarship providers at or near your school of choice who are members of the National Scholarship Providers Association (scholarshipproviders.org/page/MemberMap).

- **ACTION** - Write letters of inquiry to the scholarship providers you identified who are members of the National Scholarship Providers Association.

Chapter 5

STEP 5 - Send a "Thank You"

This is one way to set yourself apart from your competition. Appreciate each scholarship provider to which you applied. Thank them for the time and effort spent on reviewing your application. Remind the scholarship provider of how important they are as an important source of scholarship money.

One colleague did just this. He sent his "thank you" letter. He was very surprised when he got a response from the funder that said that there had been a mistake and that he should have gotten funding.

If nothing else, sending a "thank you" note will set you apart from others!

- **ACTION** - Send a "Thank You" card to every scholarship provider to which you applied, whether or not you were approved.

- **ACTION** - Send a "Thank You" card to everyone on your Support Team.

Phil Johncock, MA, MMs, GPC

Appendixes

A. Appendix A - 15 Top Eligibility Criteria Used When Choosing Scholarship Recipients

B. Appendix B - 17 Top Uses for Scholarship Money

C. Appendix C - 17 Special Services That Many Colleges Provide to Recipients

D. Appendix D - Top Scholarship Deadlines

E. Appendix E - Scholarship Do's & Don'ts

F. Appendix F - Supportive & Hindering Roles of Support Teams

Phil Johncock, MA, MMs, GPC

Appendix A - 15 Top Eligibility Criteria Used When Choosing Scholarship Recipients

Here is a list of the 15 top eligibility criteria used by scholarship providers when choosing who receives scholarship funding...

1. Academic Merit - 70%

2. Financial Merit - 69%

3. Community Service - 41%

4. Leadership - 37%

5. Higher Education Goals - 31%

6. Demographics - 31%

7. U.S. Citizen - 27%

8. Undergraduate Study - 27%

9. Intended Major - 24%

10. In-State / Local Residency - 24%

11. High School Education - 24%

12. First Generation In College - 21%

13. All Students Are Eligible - 20%

14. Specific High School - 20%

15. Public College or University - 20%

It is no surprise that academic and financial merit are the two most cited eligibility criteria. However, take a look at eligibility criteria #3-15. Many scholarship providers use other criteria to decide if you are eligible to apply and receive scholarship funding.

Source: National Scholarship Providers Association

Appendix B - 17 Top Uses for Scholarship Money

While the allowable uses for scholarship funding vary from institution-to-institution, according to the National Scholarship Providers Association, member institutions report scholarship money being used primarily for tuition and fees (79%), books and supplies (58%), room and board (45%), transportation to school and/or work (37%) and even computers (34%).

The following percentage of institutions report these 17 top uses for scholarship money:

1. **Books and Supplies - 58%**

2. Childcare - 19%

3. **Computers - 34%**

4. EFC - 26%

5. Emergencies - 16%

6. Full Cost of Attendance - 32%

7. Health Insurance - 13%

8. Loan Repayment - 11%

9. Non-School-Related Expenses - 8%

10. Professional Clothing - 11%

11. **Room and Board - 45%**

12. Student Contribution - 24%

13. **Transportation to School and/or Work - 37%**

14. Travel Domestically or Abroad - 29%

15. **Tuition and Fees - 79%**

16. Unrestricted - 26%

17. Other - 11%

Take a look again at the list above of 17 top uses for scholarship funding. Notice the unique types of uses for scholarship money, including childcare, emergencies, health insurance and even loan repayment and travel domestically or abroad.

The variety of uses for scholarship money reinforces the importance of creating a college budget and including all the expenses you anticipate needing. Please refer to Chapter 2.

Appendix C - 17 Special Services That Many Colleges Provide to Recipients

1. **Alumni Programs - 30%**

2. College Access Programming - 12%

3. College Consumer - 3%

4. College Readiness Program - 13%

5. Curriculum Assistance - 4%

6. Emergency Funding - 8%

7. Financial Aid / Literacy / Management - 14%

8. Internship Requirement - 4%

9. Job Placement Service - 4%

10. Leadership Development - 15%

11. **Mentoring Program - 29%**

12. On-Campus Social and/or Networking - 16%

13. **Online Communities (Social Media) - 20%**

14. Additional Programs and Services - 5%

15. Workforce Development - 4%

16. Wraparound Services - 13%

17. Other - 9%

Appendix D - Top Scholarship Deadlines

	Open to Public	Application Deadline	Student Notified	Student Acceptance	Award Disbursed
January	66%	15%	8%	6%	32%
February	51%	27%	7%	6%	18%
March	36%	37%	20%	13%	20%
April	23%	26%	40%	25%	18%
May	16%	13%	45%	35%	18%
June	11%	8%	36%	42%	24%
July	10%	4%	22%	41%	48%
August	20%	2%	11%	25%	59%
September	26%	5%	7%	14%	42%
October	29%	7%	7%	8%	23%
November	40%	4%	7%	8%	19%
December	45%	7%	9%	8%	34%

Appendix E - Scholarship Do's & Don'ts

Do's

- Create your Support Team (step 1). If you need help, visit CollegeScholarships.me.

- Create your College Budget (of expenses) (step 2)

- Fill out the FAFSA® form every year you're in school in order to stay eligible for federal student aid. (step 3).

- Research and apply to a variety of scholarship providers (step 4).

- Send "thank you" notes to all scholarship providers to which you applied as well as your Support Team (step 5).

Don'ts

- Don't pay attention to nay-sayers.

- Don't wait to get started.

- Parents, don't contact college financial aid officers or other officials, on behalf of a student 18 or older, without completing a FERPA form...

According to the U.S. Department of Education[77], "the Family Educational Rights and Privacy Act (FERPA) (20 U.S.C. § 1232g; 34 CFR Part 99) is a Federal law that protects the privacy of student education records. The law applies to all schools that receive funds under an applicable program of the U.S. Department of Education.

FERPA gives parents certain rights with respect to their children's education records. These rights transfer to the student when he or she reaches the age of 18 or attends a school beyond the high school level. Students to whom the rights have transferred are 'eligible students.'

- Parents or eligible students have the right to inspect and review the student's education records maintained by the school. Schools are not required to provide copies of records unless, for reasons such as great distance, it is impossible for parents or eligible students to review the records. Schools may charge a fee for copies.

- Parents or eligible students have the right to request that a school correct records which they believe to be inaccurate or misleading. If the school decides not to amend the record, the parent or eligible student then has the right to a formal

---

[77] www2.ed.gov/policy/gen/guid/fpco/ferpa/index.html?src=rn

hearing. After the hearing, if the school still decides not to amend the record, the parent or eligible student has the right to place a statement with the record setting forth his or her view about the contested information.

- Generally, schools must have written permission from the parent or eligible student in order to release any information from a student's education record. However, FERPA allows schools to disclose those records, without consent, to the following parties or under the following conditions (34 CFR § 99.31):

  - School officials with legitimate educational interest;

  - Other schools to which a student is transferring;

  - Specified officials for audit or evaluation purposes;

  - Appropriate parties in connection with financial aid to a student;

  - Organizations conducting certain studies for or on behalf of the school;

  - Accrediting organizations;

- To comply with a judicial order or lawfully issued subpoena;

- Appropriate officials in cases of health and safety emergencies; and

- State and local authorities, within a juvenile justice system, pursuant to specific State law.

Schools may disclose, without consent, 'directory' information such as a student's name, address, telephone number, date and place of birth, honors and awards, and dates of attendance. However, schools must tell parents and eligible students about directory information and allow parents and eligible students a reasonable amount of time to request that the school not disclose directory information about them. Schools must notify parents and eligible students annually of their rights under FERPA. The actual means of notification (special letter, inclusion in a PTA bulletin, student handbook, or newspaper article) is left to the discretion of each school."

For a sample form for disclosure of college records, visit this U.S. Department of Education website:

www2.ed.gov/policy/gen/guid/fpco/ferpa/safesc hools/modelform2.html

Appendix F - Supportive & Hindering Roles of Support Teams

Supportive Roles: Task & Maintenance

During the first meeting of your Support Team, it is helpful to also go over, as a group, the types of roles and behaviors that will be supportive of your Team working optimally. According the *Roles People Play in Groups* by Ann Porteus and Stanford University[78], here are two common supportive roles:

- Task Roles

- Maintenance Roles

Task Roles

"Task roles refer to the actions of individuals that help move the project, decision, task along.

Initiating

- What: Proposing task or goals; defining a group problem; suggesting procedure or ideas for getting the task accomplished.

---

[78]web.stanford.edu/group/resed/resed/staffresources/RM/traini ng/grouproles.html

- When: At the beginning of a meeting, when the meeting bogs down, or when the group needs direction or new direction.

- How: Define the task; suggest a method or process for accomplishing the task; provide a structure for the meeting.

  'It seems like we are being asked to …',
  'Does it seem like a good idea to begin by...?'

Information or Opinion Seeking

- What: Requesting facts; seeking relevant information about a question or concern; asking for suggestions, ideas or opinions.

- When: Problem solving, decision making, action planning, group discussion.

- How: Ask for more facts; collect data; seek individual opinions, ideas and suggestions.

  'What are the likely solutions?',
  'Mary, what do you think of that idea?',
  'What else do we need to know before we can proceed?'

Clarifying

- What: Interpreting or reflecting ideas and suggestions; clearing up conclusions; indicating alternatives and issues before the group; giving examples, defining terms.

- When: Any time the group discussion becomes too vague, too general or lacks focus; when a lot of information has been put out.

- How: Ask for clarification of an example; build on the ideas of others; clarify an idea based on your understanding; try to develop timid suggestions and half stated ideas into fully developed possibilities.

  'What I think I hear you saying is ___',
  'Robert, can you explain your idea a bit more,'
  'Cecilia, do you see how that idea relates to what Luis said earlier?'

Summarizing

- What: Pulling together related ideas; restating suggestions after the group has discussed them; offering a decision or conclusion for the group to accept or reject.

- When: At each transition in the meeting, when many different ideas or proposals are being considered, when the group gets off track; at the end of a meeting/ discussion.

- How: Restate the points, decisions, action plans or common themes of the discussion; remind the group of the process or method being used.

  'Let's take a minute to look at the main themes that are arising in our discussion'
  'It looks like the main points being raised are ___'
  'Remember that each person needs to offer a suggestion before we begin an open discussion.'

Consensus Testing

- What: Checking with the group to see how much agreement has been reached and how ready the group members are to consider a decision.

- When: Problem solving, decision making, action planning.

- How: Poll the group on an issue or decision to determine whether a consensus already exists.

  'Are there any objections to using creative brainstorming to identify potential solutions for our problem?'
  'Is there agreement that...?'

Maintenance Roles

Maintenance roles refer to the actions of individuals that help preserve the relationships in a group.

Encouraging

- What: Being friendly, warm, and responsive to others; accepting others and their contributions; regarding others by giving them an opportunity to contribute or be recognized.

- When: Regularly.

- How: Give recognition for contributions to the group, point out the accomplishments of the group.

    'That was a really good suggestion, Chris. Thanks.'
    'We have accomplished a lot today. Thanks.'

Harmonizing

- What: Attempting to reconcile disagreements; reducing tension, getting people to explore their differences.

- When: When the group cannot reach consensus, when conflict of ideas, opinions or personality is preventing progress.

- How: Articulate the common elements in conflicting points of view.

  'What can we do to get you to support this? What can we all agree on?'
  'We seem to be stuck. What can we do to move the discussion along?'

Expressing Group Feelings

- What: Sensing feelings, mood, relationships within the group; sharing one's own feelings with other members.

- When: When the group is having trouble making a decision, when you sense a conflict in the group, as a check-in to see how the group is doing.

- How: Verbalizing what you see as the feelings, mood, tension in the group. Openly acknowledging your own feelings about what is going on in the group.

  'I am sensing that there is some tension in the room. does anyone else feel it?'
  'It seems like some people have withdrawn from this discussion. Is that something we need to discuss?'

Gatekeeping

- What: Helping to keep communication channels open: facilitating the participation of others, suggesting procedures that permit sharing remarks.

- When: Whenever you want to hear from the more silent members of the group, whenever you want to prevent a participant from dominating the discussion.

- How: Ask an individual for their opinions or the information; be sensitive to the non-verbal signals indicating that people want to participate; when a person monopolizes the conversation, ask others for input

  'Jeff, did you want to share something?'
  'Thanks for your input, Robin. I would like to know what the rest of you think.'

Compromising

- What: When your own ideas or status is involved in a conflict, offering a compromise which yields status; admitting error, modifying ideas in interest of group cohesion or growth.

- When: When the group is stuck, when trying to make a decision and there are opposing views.

- How: Offering suggestions for getting unstuck; asking the group members to figure out a compromise.

  'I guess this method may not be the best for accomplishing this task. Shall we try Kim's idea?'
  'I feel like we are stuck with two opposing views, what can we do to reach a compromise?'

Standard Setting and Testing

- What: Checking whether the group is satisfied with its procedures; suggesting new procedures when necessary.

- When: When the group first meets together, whenever the norms that are developing prevent the group from functioning effectively.

- How: Help group define its ground rules; remind group of the standards they established for themselves anytime when those rules are ignored or broken.

  'How do we want to operate as a group?'
  'Seems like our ground rules have been forgotten. Should we take a few minutes and revisit them?'
  'I just want to remind you of the ground rules we set up in the beginning.'"

Hindering Roles

During the first meeting of your Support Team, it is helpful to go over, as a group, the types of roles and behaviors that will be a hindrance to your Team working optimally. According the *Roles People Play in Groups* by Ann Porteus and Stanford University[79], here are some common hindrance roles people play in groups and teams…

"Hindering roles refer to actions of individuals that hinder the group's process and progress.

Dominating

Behavior: Asserting authority or superiority to manipulate the group or certain members; interrupting contributions of others; controlling through use of flattery or patronization.

Solution: Establish a procedure whereby each person contributes one idea to the discussion and then must wait until every other group member does the same before contributing again; interrupt the dominator, ask him/her to summarize the point quickly so that others can add their ideas, too.

- 'Thank you for giving us all those ideas, Erin. Let's hear from others in the group now.'

---

[79]web.stanford.edu/group/resed/resed/staffresources/RM/traini ng/grouproles.html

Withdrawing

Behavior: Removing self psychologically or physically from the group; not talking; answering questions only briefly.

Solution: Do not let conflicts remain unresolved; talk with the person privately to find out what is happening; direct questions to and solicit ideas from the avoider so this person stays involved.

- 'Carol, I have noticed that you haven't been as involved in the group lately. Is everything O.K.?

Degrading

Behavior: Putting down others' ideas and suggestions; deflating others' status; joking in a barbed or sarcastic way.

Solution: When your group first gets together, review your contract and ground rules with them, highlighting the rule that all ideas will be accepted; the first time someone criticizes another person, reinforce this rule.

- 'You have a point, but we need to solve our problem, not attack each other's ideas.'

Uncooperative

Behavior: Disagreeing and opposing ideas; resisting stubbornly the group's wishes for personally oriented reasons; using hidden agenda to thwart group progress.

Solution: Incorporate statements in the original guidelines that deal with cooperation and interruptions, encourage this person to explain reasons behind his/her objection; look for any aspect of the position that supports the group's ideas so that this person moves from left to center field; refocus his/her participation as a recorder or process observer; ask the group to deal with this uncooperative behavior.

- 'It seems like we may be forgetting the ground rules we set up as a group. Should we take a few minutes to revisit them now?'

- 'Sandy, that is an interesting view. Could you explain how you came to those conclusions?'

Side Conversations

Behavior: Whispering, giggling and having private side conversations with another person.

Solution: Set guidelines and expectations at the beginning of the meeting, stop the meeting and ask those involved in the side conversation to share what they are talking about with the group, stop the meeting and comment that it is difficult for you to hear the other discussion or to concentrate on the topic at hand with side conversations occurring; privately talk with the distracters and discuss their expectations for the meeting's topics; empower others to confront the distracters with how these side conversations keep everyone from concentrating on the group's discussion.

- 'I am having trouble focusing on the discussion with the side conversations going on. Is anyone else experiencing this?'

- 'It is difficult to focus on the discussion with side conversations going on. Can we agree that we will all focus on the main discussion?'

- 'I sense we are losing people's attention and interest, can we do a check-in to see where people are on this topic?'"

About the Author

PHIL JOHNCOCK, M.A., M.MS. is an award-winning author, educator & consultant. He received scholarships to cover 100% of the costs of his bachelor's (undergraduate) and master's (graduate) degree programs.

Phil is Grant Professional Certified (GPC). He started his grant professional career in 1988 when he received a call the day after he received his master's degree. While he was flattered to be asked to write a federal grant proposal, unfortunately he had no training. "Don't worry," he was told by his future boss. "There are some videos on grant writing in the library, and there are resources here to help you."

Well, the videos put him to sleep in the first 5 minutes. And, while some resources were available, it was through interviewing successful grant writers that he learned the most in those early years.

His first Federal grant for $125,000 was successful. Expecting to serve 250 newly legalized immigrants, things changed when 500+ people showed up the first week of registration to take his classes. Luckily, he knew enough to document the need and people on the waiting list. He then went to the State of Nevada Department of Education and requested an increase in funding, which was granted.

Eventually, he received $500,000/year for 5 years and taught English and citizenship skills to over 3,000 newly legalized immigrants. The grant-funded program received national recognition. His career as a grant professional (grant writer and grant manager) was launched!

In the last 26 years, Phil has written 58 proposals, 54 which have been funded. That's a 93% success rate.

In 1993, Phil was again asked by Truckee Meadows Community College (Reno, NV) to do something he hadn't been trained to do … teach grant writing. The local community college asked Phil to teach a seminar to leaders in the local community. 45 people showed up for that first class. Throughout the course of the last 30+ years, Phil has taught over 3,000 students.

In 1997, Phil designed the first online course for the entire University and Community College System of Nevada, which also happened to be the first grant writing course ever on the Internet.

In 2001, Phil designed the first college grant writing certification program. Almost 200 students entered the program in the first two years. In 2003, he wrote and published the first of 28 books, entitled "WIN MORE GRANTS Like the Pros in 4 Steps." The book was based on research conducted as part of his 2nd masters degree thesis on the process and tips successful grant writers to be successful. The book was time-tested by hundreds of students in the grant writing certification program as well as by other teachers of grant writing.

After authoring 13 books and designing several online courses, in 2010, Phil became the Education Chair for the

Nevada Grant Professionals Association (NGPA). In this capacity, he soon realized that only 3 grant professionals in Nevada had taken and passed the Grant Professional Certified (GPC) exam. While there was indeed an interest in an online course to prepare NGPA members to pass the GPC exam, there were not enough interested Nevada folks to make putting together a course feasible.

So, Phil invited non-NGPA members to participate and designed an 8-week webinar series leading up to the GPC exam on October 5, 2011. This would allow NGPA folks to study with and learn from other grant professionals outside their state.

This led to the design and launching in 2011 of the Grant Professional Certified (GPC) Exam Prep Course Online, the first course of its kind in the world! As a result of the 8 webinar series, practice test, small group discussions, etc., 100% of the students passed the GPC Exam on their first try!

For fun, Phil enjoys ecstatic dancing and making up impromptu celebratory songs on-the-spot while playing his acoustic guitar.

CPSIA information can be obtained
at www.ICGtesting.com
Printed in the USA
BVHW041953080320
574447BV00010B/167

9 781652 020387